MINI MECHANICS

TRACTORS
AND TRUCKS

make believe ideas

MINI MECHANICS

Welcome to our **workshop.**
Meet the **crew!** We've got some
amazingly **hard-working**
vehicles in today.
Come and have a look!

Hi, I'm **Jenson Jack**, and I'm the boss!

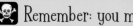 Remember: you must never play around vehicles, and tools are NOT toys!

TOOLS

grinder...

A good **mechanic** needs great tools and equipment. Take a look in our **toolbox** and find out about our favorites!

Grinders are used to cut metal.

Nuts and bolts are used to hold two or more parts together.

Jacks lift vehicles up so we can look underneath them.

....jack

nuts and bolts ......

Wrenches are used to tighten and loosen nuts.

mallet

pliers

Mallets knock out dents in vehicles.

Pliers can grip parts that are too tiny for fingers!

Gripper lamps cling to the vehicle to light up the area we are working on.

gripper lamp

Help us find the missing wrench on every page.

5

GIANT TRACTOR

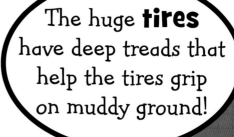

The huge **tires** have deep treads that help the tires grip on muddy ground!

Big open spaces need **monster** tractors! The biggest **tractors** have eight **wheels,** giving them amazing **grip** and **strength!**

tire

tread...

double wheels......

The world's biggest tractor is called Big Bud.

Bud is 27 ft (8 m) long, 14 ft (4 m) tall, and weighs more than ten elephants!

BIG RIG

A big rig is a mighty **truck** that has a powerful **engine** **cab** pulling one or two **trailers.** Big rigs pull anything from tanks of **fuel** to **food** supplies.

cab

Some **cabs** are so big, the drivers can sleep in them!

Massive rigs can weigh as much as 40 hippos!

The longest two-trailer rigs are as long as eight cars parked end to end!

TRACTOR

Tractors are one of the **hardest-working** machines. They are **slow,** but their big **rear** wheels give them the **super-strength** they need to **pull heavy** farm **machinery.**

engine

Small front **wheels** help tractors to turn around in small spaces.

The world record for the longest tractor wheelie is 5.3 miles (8.5 km)!

cab

The **cab** roof is designed to protect the driver in an accident.

JOHN DEERE

Machinery or trailers are attached to the **draw bar**.

wheel.........

draw bar

CEMENT TRUCK

The massive **drum** turns one way to mix the concrete and the other to push it out.

This amazing machine mixes up **cement**, sand, gravel, and water to make **concrete** on its way to the building site! Cement trucks need a crew of two - one to **drive** and one to **work** the mixer!

step........

fuel tank

The mixer's huge drum holds nearly 1.5 tons of mixed concrete -

Stickers to use on the activity pages.

Extras to stick where you want.

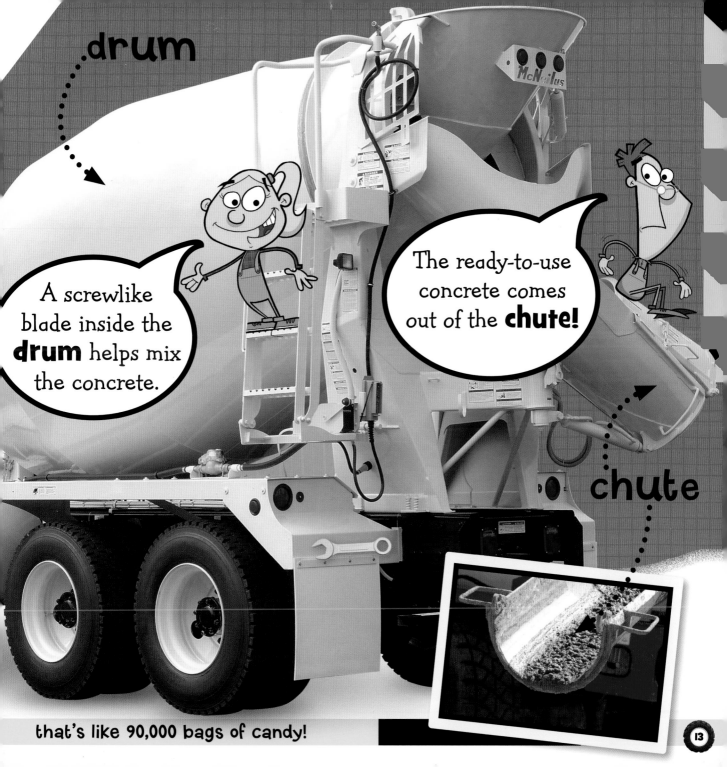

drum

A screwlike blade inside the **drum** helps mix the concrete.

The ready-to-use concrete comes out of the **chute!**

chute

that's like 90,000 bags of candy!

TOW TRUCK

A tow truck is your best friend if your car **breaks down!** It's a tow truck's **job** to **pull** vehicles out of **trouble** and take them to the nearest **garage** for **repair.**

Chains can be attached to the **links** to drag vehicles to safety.

link

292 tow trucks formed the world's longest

boom
winch

hook and
chain

The **boom** lifts vehicles up and out of a ditch!

The **hook** is attached to the vehicle being rescued.

GARBAGE TRUCK

You hear garbage trucks in the street early in the morning emptying the **trash** from homes and shops. **Stinky** but very important work!

The back of the truck opens and **hydraulic pistons** tip the hopper up to unload the trash!

This type of garbage truck is called **a rear loader.**

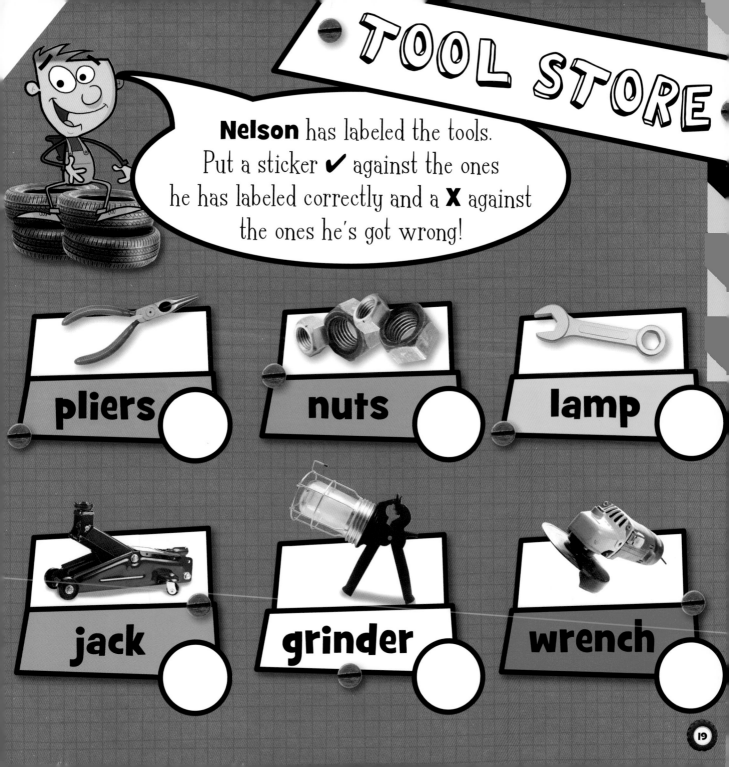

TOOL STORE

Nelson has labeled the tools. Put a sticker ✔ against the ones he has labeled correctly and a **X** against the ones he's got wrong!

pliers

nuts

lamp

jack

grinder

wrench

Great job! Now take the quiz to earn your
Mini Mechanics Gold Award!

Find stickers to complete the report.

Small front wheels help the vehicle to turn around in small spaces.

Huge tires with deep treads help this vehicle grip on muddy ground.

The massive drum turns one way to mix concrete, the other to push it out.

The mighty boom lifts vehicles up and out of trouble.

MINI MECHANICS
GOLD AWARD CERTIFICATE

This is to certify that .... has achieved the

Mini Mechanics Gold Award

for excellence in

Tractors and trucks

Sticker a star here!

Good job!